W9-BVC-779

The Culture Of Disbelief

*Gospel Sermons
For Lent/Easter
Cycle B*

Donna Schaper

CSS Publishing Company, Inc., Lima, Ohio

THE CULTURE OF DISBELIEF

Scripture quotations are from the *New Revised Standard Version of the Bible*, copyright 1989 by the Division of Christian Education of the National Council of the Churches of Christ in the USA. Used by permission.

Library of Congress Cataloging-in-Publication Data

Schaper, Donna.
    The culture of disbelief : Gospel sermons for Lent/Easter, Cycle B / Donna Schaper.
        p.   cm.
    ISBN 0-7880-1394-7
    1. Lenten sermons. 2. Holy-Week sermons. 3. Easter Sermons. 4. Bible. N.T. Gospels. Sermons. 5. Sermons, American—Women authors. I. Title.
BV4277.S33   1999
252'.62—dc21   99-16008
                                                                                           CIP

This book is available in the following formats, listed by ISBN:
    0-7880-1394-7   Book
    0-7880-1395-5   Disk
    0-7880-1396-3   Sermon Prep

For more information about CSS Publishing Company resources, visit our website at www.csspub.com.

PRINTED IN U.S.A.

*To John Vannursdall,
my friend, chaplain, and mentor,
who taught me to love the lectionary.*

Table Of Contents

You are ready to reframe your life. A new frame is a new picture, a reorientation of the material. A new frame is a kind of resurrection, or resuscitation, or renewal. It is as good as a new outfit, as fresh as a haircut that works, as lively as a well-set table awaiting a well-cooked meal.

The writer Tillie Olson spoke of her life needing margin. It had run into the walls of her frame. Artists and photographers insist that the empty space around an object defines it as much as the colored-in part. Lent is the rearrangement of the space in which we live. It is a look at context, at the air, at the nothing that is ours.

Try this exercise: Think about yourself as a still life. Put yourself in a favorite chair or window seat or grassy knoll. Paint yourself in. Use detail. Did you bring a purse? Or a basket? Or a book? Is your cat with you? How do you size up? Is the current frame appropriate? Or has it lost its paint? Are the nails coming out on the corners? Is it dirty? Dusty? Does it still interest you at all? How about the margins? Do they fit the picture? Or is the picture stranded in the margins? Or are the margins stranded by the picture? Where is the devil? Top corner? Bottom corner? In your heart? Or purse?

Jon Spayde, the writing instructor, says that a "good story lets in the little goblins." Let the devil into your picture. What does the devil want?

Then read again the story of Jesus' Temptation in the Wilderness in Matthew 4:1-11. Write a story about yourself. You have been sent to a desert for forty days. What happens to you? What three temptations come your way? Write them down. Keep the little goblins close by during Lent. Make their acquaintance. Get to know them by name. Are there angels with you also? Give them names also. Let them accompany you and your temptations.

The God of dry and lonely times, the God of powerful quiet company, the one who knows the hard times and the soft times, the good and the bad, will draw near. The more quiet we can become, the more God will be near.

When life gets old in us and we wonder if we can go on, when we mask our grief and weariness, when we refuse to look at the plight of the poor, when even Lent doesn't invite us to look in, we can still pray to the God of the quiet. We don't need to practice our piety before others. God will come to us right where we are. We do not have to be noticed by others to find God. We do not have to become vain or ridiculous on behalf of a large and grandiose spirituality. Like Jesus, we may be faithful to our daily life, just as we may be faithful to the days of our living.

Hypocrites make a "big thing" out of their Lenten reframing. They show off. They brag. And they become dismal in their bragging. Authentic Christians go quietly towards God — and are never disappointed.

In Slavomir Rawicz's book, *The Long Walk*, a Polish nobleman ends up in the wrong place at the wrong time. Stalin's army picks him up in 1944 and marches him and 3,000 other unfortunates across Siberia to a prison camp. Their labor is abused to mine the riches of the Siberian world.

They are forced into humiliation and quiet. They have no choice. On their way into Siberia, the men are chained to each other. Aboriginal Russians, riding reindeer, stop by their line. They whisper in their ears the news that their forbears have seen these marches before. Thus they are commanded to set out flint and food on their doorsteps, should the men ever desire to escape. The flint is made of dung; they teach the men how to make the fire out of dung.

Other crucial messages of hope come to the men in the line. A German, who has been keeping track of the days, sings Christmas carols on Christmas eve. The other men kill him: they don't want to hear the music. Many die on the route in to the camp.

Five men, including the nobleman, escape. They do what the short men on the reindeer tell them to do. They pick up the flint. They then march through two winters and eighteen months to their freedom in India. When the three survivors arrive, after a hellishly long walk, which involves one adventure after another, our narrator goes mad. Their story is recorded by the odd circumstance of their having seen the "snowman" of the north.

Researchers tracking the snowman get the story out of the Polish nobleman. But they could never tell the whole story of the long, quiet prayer, of the desperation of the quiet prayer, or of the way showing off could no longer matter to any of them!

Our search for a reframed life is not nearly as desperate as the journey of these heroic men. But it can be just as real. We who hunger and thirst for new life only need imitate their quiet certainty that they will get home. God is with us. Our God who sees in secret sees us all.

The Baptism Of Jesus

Mark 1:9-15

When it comes to the Christian sacraments, Baptism or Eucharist, or those beyond these two central ones, we live in a world where, "Somebody done turn the wine into water," as Jim Forbes puts it. "Somebody done turn the wine into water."

The sacraments haven't quite the power they had when the dove descended from heaven and told Jesus that God was deeply pleased with him. "This is my *beloved* son, in whom I am well pleased."

The sacraments are diluted for many of us. Instead of the straw being spun into gold, we have a situation where the gold is spun into straw. We have misuse, overuse, underuse, and abuse when it comes to the sacraments. Perhaps we can find our way to them today. We can find our way back in our own hunger for rich wine, in our own passion for gold, in our own urgencies for a blessing.

How many of us have longed for the word "beloved" from our earthly fathers or mothers! We have hungered for them. How many of us have been near jealousy for a blessing the size of a sacramental blessing! How many of us would like to know what John knew when he left the baptismal waters. Straight, he went, full of the good news of repentance for all, out to preach it to the world. Jesus' baptismal water and blessing bubbles over in John. There is nothing diluted about John the Baptist. This man is full strength.

Some scholars argue that the sacraments are a little too rich for our blood.[1] Why? Why do we dilute religious meaning at the same time that we hunger for it desperately? The answer may be

13

as simple as peer pressure. We may be looking laterally for guidance about how to bless each other, how to baptize, how to commune with each other, instead of vertically. We may be looking across, humanistically, instead of up and down, theologically. We may think the sacraments have to do with what other people see in us when we eat bread or drink wine together. We may think the sacraments have to do with having the baby "done" and how sumptuous the baptismal gown is rather than with the baby's direct relationship to a God of blessing and rich broth.

We may need to have both more privacy and less privacy in our sacramental life. At the table and at the font, it may be most important to be by ourselves with God. It may be important to forget about the congregation. Then it may also be important to return to the congregation "full" and "fully" as a person, among others, bathed in blessing.

I think of John Lasco's liturgy of public repentance in the Church of Scotland's Book of Common Order. There we pray to get beyond any sect's interpretation of the sacraments on behalf of the sacrament the One true God had in mind.

Lutherans still accuse Zwingli's people of denying the luminous nature of the Eucharist. Calvinists deplore the predominantly retrospective view of the Lord's Supper, and on and on, in a much too human conversation about what is right and wrong in the sacraments. Who cares, especially if the original blessing is denied in the argument? The dilution comes from the bickering.

A good friend wants to know why, since God created most of us as originals, so many of us come up as carbon copies? The same pattern is seen in the dilution of the power of the sacraments. Is it truly as an unknown poet argues, "The destiny of a morning star to be drowned in the clear light of noonday"? As time goes on, the shine does go off of many things.

Still, why can we not protect the Eucharist or Baptism from the dulling of time? Why can't we stay away from the bickering?

The Christian year of Advent and Lent and the Seasons of Pentecost and Trinity all but disappeared in the Reformed churches. Why? Because as the denominations fragmented into smaller and smaller groups, they couldn't agree on when to start and stop which season! Thus, we became a people who couldn't even enjoy the ashes of Ash Wednesday. Now, the Revised Common Lectionary (in which most denominations read the same texts on a three year cycle) has accelerated liturgical renewal and hymn writing, and even some Protestants wash feet on Maunday Thursday and give each other ashes on Ash Wednesday. We are inching our way back to original, sacramental observances — and God is fully prepared to receive our return!

What all faiths hope for is a renewal or reunion of Word and Sacrament, a profound linking of pulpit and table. We know that we need all the access possible to the blessing God gives us.

These lines of Philip Schaff of the Mercersburg communion, a small Reformed expression, tell of our hunger for the sacramental experience and how deep and ancient it is. In connecting our sacraments to Jewish festivals and feasts, we find ourselves much less "private" in our hunger for the sacraments. We need to go deep and wide at the same time. Deep toward God, and wide toward each other. Schaff says:

> *Christ our Passover is sacrificed for us: therefore let us keep the feast, not with old leaven, neither with the leaven of malice and wickedness but with the unleavened bread of sincerity and truth ... Present yourselves on the altar of the gospel, in union with his glorious merits. Consecrating ourselves on the altar of the gospel, in soul and body, property and life, to Thy most blessed service and praise.*

In soul and body, ancient and contemporary modes, in full connection with each other and even fuller connection with our God, we receive the sacrament.

Obviously, it is not possible to speak of degrees of Christ's presence. John the Baptist knew one degree, one level of concentration. We know another.

Theologian Hageman says, "Word and Sacrament are only different media for the same reality of Christ's coming in to the midst of his people." How does Christ come to us today? He comes in rich, original blessing, which we may find our way to by means of water, bread, wine, or just waiting for the dove. The dove wants to come and pronounce a blessing on us as well. That blessing will remind us of our baptism and send us out into the world, with the vigor of the Baptist. It will be a rich broth, especially if we receive it from God, mediated by each other.

---

1. In *Communion in Pulpit, Table and Song: Essays in Celebration of Howard G. Hageman*, edited by Heather Murray Elkins and Edward C. Zaragoza, 1996, Drew University, the point is made that the sacraments scare us.

Letting Death Go

Mark 8:31-38

Some gardeners can grow everything and others cannot. Sweet peas are a particularly difficult plant for some. They sprout two little leafs and a withered string of a hand reaching up. Then they stop growing. Something underneath is wrong. In the soil. Down deep. They don't want to live.

People who have trouble with sweet peas try over and over to grow them. They load the soil with enough chicken manure to fertilize five gardens, much less the five square feet where they'd like to see light pink and purple and sweet.

A woman who carried twins who were dead in utero and delivered at six months identifies with the sweet pea gardeners. She had the greater burden, of course. She had them in her heart but never in flower. She had them immature but never mature.

What we know about both large and small grief is that time is its healer. The pain does pass. We get "over it" by going beyond it, under, around, and through it. By March most gardeners are usually fingering the sweet pea packets on the seed rack. Couples who lose babies make love again.

What parents who lose children to premature death do is to enter their difficulty with hope. They let the grief flood them. "Let" is too active a word. The grief floods them. This way they get to its other side. What gardeners do with the many griefs in growing is the same: we swim our grief to its far shore.

When Jesus speaks of death, he speaks of its inevitability and its hope. "He said all this [about his sure and certain death] quite openly." Peter rebuked him for his openness. But Jesus knew

17

what he was doing. He was preparing his disciples for the inevitability of grief. He was assuring his disciples that his death was the will of God, because he willed it as well. He was giving up his life to gain it. Sometimes we tell parents grieving premature death that their loss is not the will of God. Surely the most offensive comment made at children's funerals is this passivity: that God somehow might have willed it. Why, such parents ask, did God will my child to enter the other side and yours not to? It is a good question, fully appropriate to the hostility of shutting down the mystery of the unfathomable. We sweep the mystery out the door, like so much dust, with the brutal broom of "must have been the will of God." The grief doesn't get to hang around, to last long enough, to find its other side.

Jesus' participation in his Father's will is different. He is letting go of life on purpose. God does not choose some children, and not others, in this way. Instead, we are all invited to be sufficiently a part of death that life can show up on the other side.

Sweet peas are grown all over the world by some people. That is a fact. In our grief, we often can't face this fact. We need to wait it out; it needs to wait us out.

The time of premature death is not a time when we need to be morally or theologically combative. But we need to be prepared. People will say, right to your face, that these things are the will of God. They are not. God does not will the death of children. God does not want gardeners who adore sweet peas not to be able to grow them. God wills life and wills it abundantly. When we understand God's will towards life, things get even more difficult to understand, at first. What we mean when we say that God does not will the death of children is that, apparently, there are some things outside of God's control — like stillborn twins and certain varieties of flowers in certain types of soil.

Both gardening and grief have an enemy. The enemy is control. This control is a matter of the heart and a matter of the will. I learned this by loving, and by amending soil with manure, and by watching a baby die. In love, and manure, and death, control is the thing we have to fear most. Manure the garden. Manure it completely. But don't extract guarantees of life from the soil. The soil can't give the guarantees.

A nursery school teacher said that when something hurt her it hurt in the heart and it was her heart that got swollen. A child reported that she was so sad inside that her heart was going to burst. The teacher didn't understand the child right away until she remembered her metaphors. Once we get into the right language, we can communicate. The teacher consoled the child with the news that hearts were the one thing that could swell up really bad but not get broken — not burst apart. The teacher is right. The teacher speaks truth.

Swollen, yes; burst, no. Swollen, not broken. Heart, not will. The will can crack. The heart can't. God is the same. It was after all a Son who died in Jesus Christ. Surely that was in a place of the swollen heart, not a cracked will. No God would willfully kill a son, or make a sweet pea impossible. But a Son could choose to participate in suffering on behalf of his own and our larger life.

While waiting for the soil to improve and the right time to return for babies, we can do one more thing. While waiting for the chance to say yes to suffering, on behalf of life (*not on behalf of suffering*), we can just be there, stand there, do nothing, make thin remarks, or sound stupid even to ourselves.

When showing up at the sight of grief, often we are afraid we won't have the right thing to say. And our fear is correct. We will not have the right thing to say. But still we can show up, and stand there, and say nothing. Or say that we know nothing to say. But still we are here, swollen heart and all, but not broken by our wordlessness.

A minister stood in the hospital waiting with a mother to find out if her seven-year-old's spleen was as divided as the doctor said it was. It was. His mother didn't find out until morning. Her grief has swollen like an ocean after a hurricane so many times since that night of the long wait for the bad news. Up and down. Down and up. In and out. Sometimes she would just show up at the minster's office and say, "Just a hug," that's all, "Just a hug." Hugs and hugs later, we do get over these things. But we also never forget.

We imagine seven-year-olds hanging on a bar, hanging upside down, safe. The facts contradict this possibility. The car crash was a mild one. Matthew and his mother walked away from it. Eight hours later he died from a spleen cut in two. His father held him in his arms and watched him die.

This much I believe about heaven: fathers hold children in arms there. Sweet peas grow. Don't ask me how. There the children are different; they don't age. They hang upside down on bars in eternal agility. The soil is rich. Even the Ninja Turtles are different, more mellow, less violent. Connection — the hug — is there. Its reality is the eternal part.

One more thing that we learn from death. We must remember to mind the other children, the siblings, the lives ones, the ones who still have bodies. Gardeners who can't grow sweet peas have to pay attention to what they can grow.

With Matthew, there was a sister. Heather. She was seventeen at the time of the accident. She and Matthew had come from Korea together. She was entering her senior year in high school. Her parents were facing the empty nest suddenly. Not only would Matthew be gone but in one year Heather would be gone. Imagine the sheer work it took for her parents not to smother Heather. She might have stayed out of college for one year. "No," they said "love lets go; it doesn't hold on."

In *Angels In America*, a play about AIDS, the playwright Kushner says:

> *If we are to be visited by angels we will have to call them down with sweat and strain, we will have to drag them out of the skies, and the efforts we expend to draw the heavens to an earthly place may well leave us too exhausted to appreciate the fruits of our labors: an angel, even with torn robes, and ruffled feathers, is in our midst.*

Christ as an angel is closer to what my faith can see than Christ as a baby or Christ as a sweet pea. Angels come down from above;

flowers and babies grow up. God was with Jesus in a way "deeper" than God is with us. This relationship is on a spectrum. Jesus was also with God in a way "deeper" than we are with God. God sends grief, but God does not will our grief. There is a difference.

Grief is a part of the great unfathomablity. Great grief comes to the same world that receives great joy. Children are such great joy. We don't deserve them, can't control them, dare not crush them with our own fear, must let them go.

Our hearts will swell, but they will not break. Even if our flowers don't all grow, we are still invited to let them be. So that we may also let what can grow to, in fact, grow.

Turning The Tables

John 2:13-22

A man feared his wife was going deaf. He tried an experiment. He placed himself at one end of a large room and began to whisper to her, "Can you hear me?" No answer heard. He moved to the middle of the room. "Can you hear me?" No answer heard. He got right next to her and said, "Can you hear me?" "For the third time," said she, "yes, I can hear you."

The wife had turned the tables on her caring husband. He thought she was deaf. In fact, it was he.

Jesus turns the tables of the entire world! He shows us that we can look at ourselves and our own disabilities, that we don't need to look at others so much. He cleanses the Temple by throwing out the money changers and overturning their tables. He lets people know that "his Father's House" will not be run by the rules of the marketplace. It will be run by a different set of rules — a turning of the table set of rules.

Many of us approaching the end of the century hunger for a different set of rules. We long for a jubilee experience, the kind the Israelites had from time to time, in which all debt was cancelled, all the land redistributed, all sins forgiven. Every seven years, from whence comes our sense of "sabbatical," things were evened out.

Wouldn't it be wonderful to even out our personal lives? To turn the tables over and start again? To let go of the mistakes we did make, the hopes we forgot, the dreams we destroyed? Wouldn't it be fun every seven years, or even seventy years, to have another chance at this thing called life?

23

Wouldn't it be fun to be out of the clutches of the "eye for an eye and tooth for a tooth" crowd? To stop paying off our credit card debt with new credit cards? Not to owe any more but to have the slate wiped clean? To live in a world not ruled by the accountants and the money changers, the liars and the thieves?

Just such fun is what Jesus offers in his unusual anger at the money changers in the Temple. He offers something new. He shifts the paradigm. He says that the rules are not what they seem. We do not pay for everything. Some things, like the Temple, live in a place beyond the change rate.

Things are made new, by Jesus, using the Temple. It may be destroyed, he says. But it will be raised up. The new rules are more real than the old rules.

Jesus is not talking about only shifting our mental paradigms. He means to turn the real tables as well. If Jesus were to rise today, he would rise in global debt resolution. He would resolve global debt, both metaphorically and actually. He would forgive debt so that Ugandans could pay seventeen dollars per person on health care and three dollars per person on foreign debt, instead of the exact opposite, which they do today. He would rise from the death of debt. New life is very real to those who know the cancellation of debt. Visit an AA meeting any night of the week, in any community in America. You will hear the stories of cancelled debts. These debts are not imagined; they are real. So is the resurrection.

The resurrection of Jesus is connected to Israel's Year of Jubilee as a practical solution to the sins of the world. Jubilee frees hopelessly indebted people the way bankruptcy frees an individual. It creates new land and new time. Freeing hopelessly indebted countries from all debt without condition is what Jesus claims to have done by his death on the cross. Debt is canceled in new life.

The only reason not to cancel the debt of two-thirds of the world is the hoarding and false self-interest of the already rich. The reasons to cancel it include hundreds of thousands of children around the world, whose parents did not engage the debt their children will be buried in. Most debt was contracted by authoritarian or military regimes: the people now "paying" the debt did not sign up for their monthly fees. They are not responsible for the debt they cannot, at any rate, pay.

C. S. Lewis pictured Christ as a lion named Aslan in his famous children's series about the land of Narnia. Aslan is not a tame lion. He has a way of bursting out of the spiritual closets in which we lock him. He shows up in ghettoes and in banks.

Jesus comes into the Temple to change the world's tables. He is always speaking the same message, no matter how far away in the room we are from him. For the third and fourth time, have we heard him yet? I wonder.

I wonder who is really deaf. I wonder what would happen to the children of the world and the temples if we were to hear the sound of tables turning over. It might sound a lot like the rolling away of the stone!

Jesus is shifting the understanding of the temple or the understanding of what we now call church in this text. He is shifting the paradigm. As Walter Brueggeman puts it, there are at least three First Testament images for "church." One is the Davidic or temple-based people, another is wilderness, and the third is alternative community.[1] We talk a lot about wilderness — but may actually be moving out of wilderness into an alternative community. With regard to money and numbers in the church today, we don't act alternative so much as we act temple!

Jesus throws the money changers, the bean counters, out of the Temple. He is asking the people of God to live from an alternative basis. We are being asked to live by new rules, rules beyond the old rules of exchange and tit for tat.

Rhea Miller explores the new physics and the new biology.[2] The old science, or clenched fist, is a concept of rigidity; the cloudhand represents more of what the new science thinks things really are. Every moment in the trace is different: at the basis of matter, the new physicists tell us, is flow and movement.

Cloudhand is the real basis of matter or ontology, not Darwin's "survival of the fittest." The new biology of Lynn Margulis and Dorion Sagan, who insist that survival came within the context of, and is dependent upon, community or cooperation, joins the new physics of Heisenberg's "Uncertainty Principle" or Mandelbrot's problem in measuring a coastline, which he decided changed too much ever to be measured. Chaos is real, even friendly.

It may be that the main purpose we have as the century ends/ begins is to change the way we think about the diffusion of the gospel. It may be that thought needs to change as much as purpose. According to Miller:

> *Paradigm shift is a word meant to convey the changing of the way we view the world: the turning or shifting of our perception, our overall concept of reality. It is not so much a matter of a change in the content of our world as it is a shift in our understanding. It is not so much a change of pitch on a musical scale, as a change in tone ... It is how the facts fall into a new place for us ... it is important to understand that a paradigm shift is not a matter of seeing things more clearly. Rather, it is like perceiving the universe in a different color ... a paradigm shift does not negate what has gone before ... former scientific knowledge is not so much incorrect as inadequate....*[3]

Miller also knows how to teach the foundations of the new science, which is "pattern recognition."[4] We are connected to each other, in our patterning, and also distinct, because "if each of us is true to our own unique unfolding or 'emergence' our paths will not cross or negate one another's."[5] Think of the cloudhand. "It is precisely when we try to control our paths, to copy or model our path on someone else's ... that our paths suddenly become destructive."[6]

How do we change the tables and live by new rules? We find power in the cloudhand theory of patterned irrepeatability. One very tiny difference can change an entire pattern. Weather people call this the "Butterfly effect." (It is not lost on Miller, or others, that the weatherman who discovered the butterfly effect, Edward Lorenz, also developed a "Lorenz attractor," a computer generated image of a chaotic system, that resembles the cloudhand.) In theory, the air disturbed by the wings of a butterfly can and does change the weather around the world. Little things mean a lot, or as Jacques

Maritain put it: "The means are in a sense the end in process of becoming."[7]

For Miller, Jesus was a paradigm buster. He used parables, which depend on paradox, to break through the normal religion of his time. His purpose was to break open the worldview parameters. "Parable is paradox at work." [8] Jesus turns the tables. This is Jesus making all things new; parable and paradox are the methods he uses.

---

1. Walter Brueggeman, "Images of the Church," *Theology Today* (Spring, 1991).

2. *Cloudhand, Clenched Fist: Chaos, Crisis, And The Emergency Of Community* by Rhea Y. Miller (Luramedia), 1996.

3. *Ibid.*, p. 31.

4. *Ibid.*, p. 71.

5. *Ibid.*, p. 113.

6. *Ibid.*, p. 117.

7. In "L'Homme et l'Etat," quoted by James Douglas in *The Nonviolent Coming of God* (Orbis), p. 154.

8. Miller, p. 117.

Paying Attention To The Modern Light

John 3:14-21

We were all asked to bring our church's Bibles to the annual meeting of the Association as part of the liturgy. Dozens of parishes placed their old leather tomes on the altar. They stacked them in a criss-cross way. One man came forward with a laptop computer. He opened its face and plopped it on top of all the old leather.

A strange "ah" moved through the congregation.

Many of us are sure that God is a part of these changes and at least one step ahead of the devil. We know that an on-line Bible is as good as a printed one. We know that even cyberspace has a heaven and a hell. Human beings manage technology and the result is that we can accomplish both good and evil through it.

One gay student at a large and impersonal state university met his college chaplain on-line. He had been doing confidential Bible study with a campus chaplain on-line. When he became suicidal, he turned to his on-line chaplain. Without ever meeting each other, the student walked back from his brink. The Holy Spirit, not the chaplain, carried him back to life.

Those of us who know the pattern of the Holy Spirit are not surprised. We know how Spirit breaks through nooks and crannies, webs and nets. We know how Spirit gets where it wants to get.

Another student woke his father early one morning. "Dad, wake up. I have to talk to you." After fumbling and coffee and seats at the kitchen table, the sixteen-year-old told his father, "I have been having a relationship with a woman on-line. She is a

Yale student; she is a beauty queen; she plays varsity tennis. Dad, when she asked me to say more about myself, I lied to her. I told her I was a Dartmouth student, a star athlete, a 4.0 student. Now she wants to meet me. What am I going to do?"

The father smiled before he told his son all he knows about the human race. "What makes you think she has been telling the truth about herself?" The son, from his naivete, responded, "Oh, Dad, she would never do that."

The Holy Spirit is working the net. But it is working it in the same ways it works every other human medium. Sometimes we allow the Spirit to do good; other times our own delusions get in the Spirit's way. Often we are too naive to know the difference.

How will we know the good from the bad? Saint Paul's fruits remain the answer. We will know the good from the bad by the degree to which the Holy Spirit uses the newer technologies for good. Does light come through or is darkness the result of our connections on-line? That is the key question. The author of John understands: today's text points us to the differences between light and darkness, either ancient or modern. There is little difference. In goodness, more people are more well off. More people connect to each other in positive, non-abusive ways. Faith increases. Hope is greater. People's hands are not stomped as they climb out of the well of history and despair. Light overwhelms darkness; the fruits of the technology are good.

In modern cyberspace we have to pay special attention to find the light. Just like the innocent sixteen-year-old, many of us are having a love affair with cyberspace. We can't imagine it would ever lie to us or hurt us! But it may. It could. Cyberspace is not supra-human. It is a human artifice, a thing made with hands, out of the mind of human beings. Cyberspace is neither good nor evil: humans are both, and that is why we may both love it and watch it with great care.

Where do we get this kind of permission to scrutinize the modern world? To keep it under the Bible, rather than letting it bury the Bible? Where do we get the permission to see deeply into the net and see the Holy Spirit there? We get it from the entrance of God into history through Jesus Christ.

"And this is the judgment, that light has come into the world." Because the light of God has come into the world, we speak of what we know and testify to what we have seen. We have seen below, beneath, under, and around and through our own times! We are not fooled by the lies the computer may sometimes tell us, or that we may tell on the computer ourselves.

Cyberspace threatens to democratize human existence or to tyrannize it, depending on who gets control. Either way, the webs and nets will have enemies. Alertness to the passage of the genuine Holy Spirit on the web may save these technologies, if anything can.

Paying attention to the movements of the Holy Spirit (or Spirits) on the net will involve the use of spiritual power and spiritual discernment. We will need to ground ourselves in the breakfast father who warns his son that not everything that looks true and good is true and good. We will need to be even more Pauline in our approach to cyberspace than we are in our approach to normal powers. Why? Because cyberspace has powerful capacities. It is even larger in its potential for good and evil than the spaces we have known.

Can we always see the light? No. Can we always hear it? No. But there it is. Unexpected light we might call it. The light makes us unexpectedly light as people. We don't carry our fear around. We are not heavy. We are light.

We blend what others call *reality* with God's reality. We make God the center of our time and place.

The text in John that we serve today is very harsh on those who do not see the action of God in their time and place. It calls those who miss God's action, the people of darkness, or the people who love darkness more than they love light.

A friend of mine swears the purpose of his life is to catch God in the act. It is not a bad purpose. God will be caught in the act as the century turns. God will be caught in the act on the Internet and in the Honduran revolutions of the world. God will be caught in the act of your day, this day, no matter how small it may seem to you. Those able to see will see. Those who are blinded by their own darkness will not be able to see.

The action of God is silent enough to miss! But it is sure enough, as well. Lean towards the light. God will be there. We can only speak of what we know, and only testify to what we have seen. Every little bit we see, let us speak. Our testimony will help others see; it will be part of the unexpected light of God, which will make us unexpectedly light!

Discerning light from darkness is part of our God-given human choice-making capacity. We turn on. We turn off. We have to be very careful that we know not only how to turn on but also how to turn off. Our awe at technology needs to be grounded in larger awes. We need a hermeneutic of suspicion or cautious trust with regard to all sacred texts, including the computer and the old leather tome.

The awe that many of us experience in cyberspace is a beautiful awe — we have to make sure that we don't get cowed by it, that our awe does not make us feel small or stupid but rather expansive and connected. Awe can go to idolatry awfully quickly.

An example of the kind of silence that may be necessary, from time to time, is available from Honduras. The Honduran newspaper *Siglo Veinte Uno* refused to print May 31 and June 1, 1993. Their motto is, "After the word, silence is the second greatest force in history." Their silence was their protest of the tyrannical coup that had happened in their country. They published all blank pages. While I would not imagine going on-line and saying nothing, I could imagine just listening in. I could imagine greater degrees of consent in the use of our new technologies. I could imagine protesting certain forms of garbage that occupy the net and not just the pornographic ones. Some of the stuff coming on is vulgar and profane by virtue of its stupidity, as well as its pornography.

Silence in cyberspace? Or silence off cyberspace? The maximization of choice is the way to make cyberspace beautiful and to guarantee its fruits. For choice to exist genuinely, we have to be able to go "silent" in cyberspace as well as to make noise.

For Christians, the virtues of cyberspace may be judged best by how Christlike they permit and help us to be. Christ, incarnate, is oddly the "right" size for a human, not too small as in "worm" and not too big as in "god." Light has a better chance when human beings get their sizes right.

Virginia Owens puts this criteria well in her excellent book titled *Selling Jesus In The Modern Age*. She asks, "What sign of *Christ* will be left behind when this age is over?" Some of the signs will surely be on-line. She argues on behalf of the beautiful art of places like Chartres or artifacts like those of Turkey or music like Bach and wonders if perhaps the age of the Christian is already over. I disagree. The Holy Spirit can surely penetrate cyberspace. That involvement is easier than building Chartres was.

Given the size of the world's population and the burden of knowledge of our interacting complexity, access to webs and nets is a brilliantly pro-human, pro-communion technology — depending on who controls it and how they control themselves while controlling it. God does have more light to shine forth — and computers can join Bibles in letting the light shine.

That computer sits on top of those old Bibles, not because it is their superior but rather because it is a part of their work. They are different modes with which to tell the same story, the story about heaven and hell, light and darkness, and how we may hope to spend more of our life times in one than the other.

The Troubled Heart Of Jesus

John 12:20-33

Jesus is beginning in this text, at this point of his ministry, to tell us he is not kidding about the suffering he will see. "He told all of this to indicate the kind of death he was to die." The kind of death he was to die. It is not a good day. The disciples see that he is troubled. He is talking with God. He has begun the small doubt that he was to know. What shall I say? Shall I speak to my father?

He does. A voice comes, confirming his death and the glorification that will come from it. "... when I am lifted up from the earth, I will draw all people to myself." We are assured that Jesus will have a victory through his death. "Now the ruler of this world will be driven out." Who is the ruler of this world? Some say the devil. I say indifference. I might even say that the devil *is* indifference.

Consider what is going on in your community right now. It is probably not much different than what is going on in my community.

I think of the closing of one of our large hospitals. A newspaper editorial tried to wake people up: "The roof has fallen in on City Hall! The Cathedral's windows have been broken! South Church's steeple fell down! The Pioneer Valley Central Labor Council's megaphone, microphone, and phone systems went out! Disaster has struck the city!"

Most people thought they were talking fiction, like Andrew and Philip did at first, also. They were not really talking fiction. Only sort of. A big and good local hospital closed. A large local factory also moved to Mexico. No big deal, we might say. Only a continuation of a lingering, smoldering fire that has charred the economic infrastructure of my town and your town and is now taking its hits on the moral and political infrastructure as well. The silence is deafening: paychecks disappear! People turn their gaze.

What Jesus asks by the glory of his death is that we accept his permission to bother. To notice. To see. To lament. To care. These are religious motions. If we do not make these moves, their capacity dies in us. If we are not able to move and be moved religiously, we die also. More of our local communities may already be more dead than any of us dare admit.

There is no glory in death when indifference rules the city. There is glory in the death of love. Watch why Jesus dies: not to validate the ruler of the world in cynicism and hatred and indifference. He dies, rather, to defeat the ruler of the world by a larger love.

Notice closed hospitals. Many close without giving appropriate legal notice to employees. Many are penalized for violating the WARN act, an early advisory system to protect employees who are about to be "canned." The safety net would be just fine if there weren't so many holes in it. It is ragged at best. Bother. Notice. See. Lament. Care. Jesus would have.

Can you imagine what it was like to be a limboed lay-off on each of these days? Or to be a teenager in that family? Or a spouse? Or the bank holding the mortgage on the 3-bedroom, nice back-yard home? Or the parish awaiting its pledge?

Noticing is not whining. Noticing is caring. What can we do to stop the damage to our lives, our paychecks, our children, our dignity? Our Jesus?

We can notice. We can make the lines hum with possibility and indignation. We can also care. We can refuse the destruction of our economic, political, and moral environment sitting down.

The root word to salvation is security, shalom, safety. Religious communities are about the business of salvation, not the business of business. But salvation is on a continuum. Genuine Divine Providence wants people to be fed, to have good work, to be able to pay their bills. Salvation and security shake hands with each other in justice.

The glory of Jesus Christ is his death on a cross on behalf of salvation, against the ruler of the world, the one we call hate and indifference, if we're too afraid to use the devil word itself.

Many people have had childhoods surrounded with anxiety about jobs. Many people still live with anxiety about their next pay check. The roof falls in on their city hall. The spires of their churches fall down.

Is there a way people can join Philip and Andrew in hearing about what kind of death people will suffer? Can your town or city hear? Notice? Care? See? Lament? Before it is too late to really help? Before it is too late to fix the roof and right the steeple. Before Providence takes any more hits.

What glorified Jesus' death is the way he died. His "Heavenly Father," as he called him, said, "I have glorified ... his death, and I will glorify it again." Somehow I don't believe Jesus died only once on the cross. I think Jesus dies every time someone gets hurt and others don't care.

I believe we have a chance to be part of the glory of the cross. Maybe we don't have big dramatic hospital closings as our cross. But I'll bet a boy was suspended from school and no one noticed. I'll bet a young girl was killed by a drunk driver and people's fuel of love for her family ran out the first week. I'll even bet something bad happened to one of you and no one noticed.

See. Bother. Lament. These are the actions of caring. They glorify the cross. Jesus knows. He led the way. His heart did not stay troubled. His love started out in a troubled way. By the action of caring, Jesus defeated the deviltry of indifference. He also lifted himself up from the trough of trouble into the glory of hope. He led the way out of the trough: he led the way to glory. We may follow — by seeing, by bothering, and by lamenting. These are the routes to glorification.

Working With Jesus At Bethany

Mark 14:1—15:47

An arrogant young woman wired home from her new job, "Made supervisor, feather in my cap." A few weeks later they got a wire, "Made management, feather in my cap." Then after another month, they got a wire, "Fired. Send money for ticket to fly home." Her parents wired back, "No ticket necessary, use feathers."

In the story of the anointing at Bethany, Christians behave in ways that many Christians have forgotten how to behave. One Christian is extravagant. She is "wasteful." She gives from the heart. The disciples want to know why the woman with the alabaster jar of ointment didn't sell it and give the money to the poor. Jesus explains: "I am going to die, very soon. That's why."

Surely some had not realized how numbered his days were. But the woman with the ointment knew. She knew she didn't have many more chances to anoint her Savior. She was a completely different character than our rich young woman of the feathers. She lived for something more than her own effect on the world. She lived for Jesus.

Many of us have become the victims of our own feathers and our own pragmatism. We are so committed to efficiency, and productivity, and saving the poor, that we rarely remember why we are so driven in these directions. As right as it is to work hard for the poor, and to have an impact on the world, it is even more right to remember Jesus. And to remember, especially on this day of the Palms, how brief a time we had him with us.

39

Some of you probably know another famous biblical woman, named Martha. She is always complaining about how overworked she is. The First Shift at the job. The second shift at home. The third shift complaining to you about the first and the second shifts. She paradoxically hates work but believes in it anyway. Her complaints are actually self-praise: her hyperactivity is her ticket to community approval.

Some of you probably also know Mary. Mary is just the opposite of Martha. When people talk about her, they describe her as lazy, and it's not just the soap operas in the afternoon, the art work in the morning, or her somewhat spacy but apparently contented children. Mary threatens people. Sometimes she actually looks like she is having a good time.

Mary is more likely to have "wasted" her nard on Jesus. Martha would die with it still locked away in a cupboard, along with the "good" china, which never got used.

I wish this conflict between pragmatic work and praiseful work was reserved only for women who also happen to be wives and mothers. It is not so reserved.

When a man loses his job, people in this country go berserk for at least two reasons. We fear his loss of income, and we also fear his loss of self-esteem. We are all of us afraid that men without jobs will know no approval. We must be *effective* to have approval in this world. Since there is not enough to go around, we had better hang on to what we have. We have an "oil crisis."

If we think we need feathers in our cap, we will find it very hard to live without them. Our culture in fact is one that lives ethically in the dregs of the Protestant work ethic. Middle class men and women live by its lights instead of those of Christian grace, not to mention poor people who are beaten over the heads with these so-called lights almost daily. Why are they poor? Because they won't work. Because they are lazy. Even though most of the women are mothers of young children. Still, the poor are poor because they won't work.

But work is not the basis for our salvation! Grace is. At the deepest downest part of things, grace is real. The work ethic is phony. What matters is the way we praise God. If we may praise

God extravagantly, and spend all that we have that way, we can be saved. If we cannot, we can only save, and hoard. Our cupboards will be full, but our hearts will be empty.

The work ethic is the devil's work: it took something good, like work, and turned it into something bad, like control. The anointer at Bethany didn't try to control life: she tried to spend her life, for Jesus.

The work ethic is a semi-sophisticated ploy to control God, to make God do our bidding. The work ethic didn't start that way, but it has become a sacrifice laid at an altar, a way to appease God, a goat, a lamb, a burnt offering.

The work ethic began more innocently. It began as that rather firm and particularly American belief that if we work, things will go well for us, and if we don't, they won't. Now, we argue that if they don't go well for us, it is probably our fault for not working. The God who is implied by the Protestant work ethic is mean: he needs sacrifices laid at the altar daily. Paystubs. Raises. Promotions. Upward mobility. A well-feathered cap.

The God we actually worship in Jesus is a God who requires none of these sacrifices. Rather our God receives gifts, in the form of expensive oil and in the form of praise and play.

In the beginning, the Protestants did not mean the hyperactivity of modern sacrifice. They meant only to experience the grace of God deeply enough so that they could make and do, buy and sell, trade and travel. They thought that material prosperity might be a sign of their election by God to renew and remake their world. Capitalist activity was an offering to God. Since the Reformation, capitalist activity has become a sacrificial, controlling offering. God has been nudged out and off the serious stage. Now, we are human doings not human beings. We make and do and make and do and don't feel elected so much as oppressed. We are busied to death.

We accumulate to our own death. We dare not spend for fear that we might come up empty — when in fact if we were to spend what we have, we would come up full!

Our worship of pragmatism has made us hyperactive. The hyperactivity is not just ecclesial. It is not just pastors or priests who lay their appointment book on the altar. It is also corporate executives, housewives, labor organizers, social activists, and medical doctors. Very few people have any memory of what it is like to play, to do what you want to do rather than what you have to do. The woman at Bethany played with Jesus: she did what she wanted to do!

Many working people can't consider giving church a shake because they are too far removed from the holy, which for them is relief from the prod; time out of the saddle; time at a kid's soccer game, even if it is Sunday morning; time off; not time on. It is what some might call grace and what others might call ointment.

What is this story telling us about the value of our buying and selling? "Why was this ointment wasted in this way? For this ointment could have been sold for more than three hundred denarii, and the money given to the poor." Can't you just hear the self-righteous envy of the disciples? She did what they couldn't do. She spent. She gave. She refused either to buy or sell.

What can God possibly be saying to us about the human economy? Neither buying or selling is directly related to our reward, not on heaven and not on earth. Mary slept late this morning, and it's okay with God. God is affirming your teenage son's approach to his summer job. God is saying that the number of grapes picked is enough. God is siding with the siesta people against the short coffee break people. God is siding with the extravagant.

There is no salvation worth having that we can earn. We can play our way to salvation instead of earning it. Play is anything you want to do; work is anything you have to do. Some people can play at faxing memos to the office from the campsite; other people can't. Play does not mean that we quit our jobs tomorrow and move into our couches. Play is an attitude: a spirituality, a home — spiritual home. It has to do with what stands inside us when we tell the boss we've had enough. Play is a freedom. Play is truly a feather in our caps — lightness.

Play is the ability to give away what we have. Play is the ability to give away what we have in the face of what to some is the ultimate scarcity, death. Play plays with death. It anoints it. It does not see it as scarcity or ending time. Play understands what

42

Jesus understood: time and life go on after death. There is an eternity to life. We can and may enjoy each other now, even if there is not much time left.

Play, many fear, is not plausible. What is not plausible in the terms of the gospel is the world of works righteousness. What is not plausible is neglected children, ozone depletion, white collar slavery, and women folding ironing at midnight. That is what is not plausible. Grace is more plausible than work any way you look at it.

Ask the people who, every now and then, sneak out of the office building and the kitchen, and remember what it was supposed to be like from the beginning. *Solo Gratia. Solo Fide.* We are saved by grace alone. Some of us take off early on those days. And others of us never go on, even though you can find many of us sitting at our desks or folding our ironing. We don't live a switched life, turn me on, turn me off. We play at work. We play with our God. Sometimes we just play with our feathers.

And surely, if we are lucky enough to run into Jesus at Bethany, we give him all that we have and are.

Junk Food And Holy Tables
Or The Cup Of Good Friday

John 18:1—19:42

Bread and wine go with communion the way turkey goes with Thanksgiving. They belong to each other. They are the proper menu for the culture from which they spring. Bread and wine spring from the Christian culture, where a little is a lot, a small man is a great man: Christianity is a place where memory is the foundation of hope.

It is no accident that Jesus initiated the Lord's Supper from within the Passover tradition. The memory of so many Passovers became the foundation for the early Christians of communion. Nor is it any accident that Jesus spoke of cups when his time of suffering came: he saw the cup of blessing as the cup of suffering. They were the same cup to him.

From time to time, youth groups "do" communion with popcorn and soda. Young couples have pasta for Thanksgiving. These methods of exempting ourselves from the rules of the feast are lots of fun for youth. If fifty-year-olds are still exempting themselves from the table manners of their group, they become what Toni Morrison calls a "spectacle." They don't tell the truth of the culture or themselves.

Morrison says a truth is the story ritual tells; spectacle adorns lies. Eucharist says that a central Christian truth is feast at the table of God. Eucharist means God with us in food. Eucharist is bread and wine in Christ or Messianic disguise. The Holy Spirit dresses the table. The cup is both a blessing and a suffering.

Many argue that what keeps Americans from genuine ritual, and so capable of grotesque spectacle, is that we are still trying to

45

act "different." We are still children. American exceptionalism runs deep. We don't think we need the feast that most other peoples enjoy when they celebrate holidays. We think we can get by without holy food. We also think we can get by without suffering.

A wise activist said that she wasn't sure which had done more for justice, Catholics refraining from meat on Fridays or soup kitchens. Ritual is powerful in the way it shapes a people. If a people is not shaped by feast at table with God as really present, then the people remain juvenile, undeveloped, pre-truth as opposed to truthful. Vatican II managed to turn the matter of Real Presence into a theological controversy — as though people didn't understand metaphor in their own pre-critical ways. We know what real presence means; we don't need to argue about its truth. We experience it at table, not the way theologians tell it, but in our own ways. We feel God at the ritual table. We experience God in the feast, and we experience God in the absence of feast, in our own suffering.

When asked once how to preach the gospel, a wise man said, "Use words, if necessary."

Our culture is in its youth about food, both our holy food and our regular food. We are immature in our table manners. We are immature in our understandings of the very blessing that comes with and through and after suffering.

We eat out of bags, even at church potlucks, which used to be food heaven and now are linked to efficiency the way almost everything else is. We come together for community and "bring our own." Fast food is about as close as we get to holy food. Since fast is what we worship, it should be no surprise that our food's rituals come out of disposable bags.

I think in contrast of a very poor woman I once knew who had three children. Many nights she served them pork and beans on a tattered linen table cloth. She knew the holiness of food.

In the '50s, women's magazines advocated the recipe that could be prepared in sixty minutes. Now quick chicken recipes reign. Ten minutes is the maximum time a dish may take to be prepared. Many deacons in my denomination spend precious hours deciding how to make sure the communion doesn't take "too long." That attitude towards feast and thanksgiving — "Euchariste" — tells all. It tells that time is what we worship, not God at table with us. It is the real reason many of our Protestant communions are spectacles, not rituals. They only pretend to worship God. Major religions have always linked food and faith. Bernard Glassman in *Instructions To The Cook: A Zen Master's Lessons In Living A Life That Matters* (Bell Tower, 1996) encourages us to eat. Last year he held a Passover Seder for homeless men in New York City's Bowery district. He sees Zen as nothing more, or less, than the art of eating a good meal. In a good meal, we throw nothing away. We use what we have. We recognize our faults as our best ingredients. Eucharist joins Seder in linking our daily intake to our long term output. We are what we eat.

I was helped to understand the Eucharist by an article in the *Boston Globe* (July 21, 1996) by Mark Rosenthal, titled "Ten Reasons Why it's So Hard to Change our Eating Habits (and three reasons why we might)." There are more obstacles in our way than we normally observe. Habits run very deep, with religious habits and assumptions having an uncanny resemblance to that reach for the potato chip than we might want to understand. That reach is Pauline — the good that I would do, I don't do, and the evil that I would not do, I do!

Protestants continue being the way we've been even though we lose members, trip over our own secularism, idolatrize culture's own prizes, and become, in the words of one of our chief critics, increasingly "dispensable" and "disposable." We eat junk food.

Gluttony is a national tradition. "All you can eat" is a First World hyphenation. No wonder one third of the population is overweight. Public health messages are off the mark; they are punitive and frightening and fad driven. The politics of agriculture corrupt the way we eat. There is more corporate profit in unhealthy food than in healthful food. The truth of our food is deep within our economic system; our attachment to food as "product" is what we ritualize daily in the way we buy to eat.

Rosenthal's ledger is full on the negative side and lightweight on the positive side. He says the three reasons we might change are that environmental pressures may alter our diet, the medical establishment may enter the fray, and some have already started to improve our eating habits, "sort of." These economic hopes make slim pickings for "hungry, dry bones, can these stones become bread" people! We search for good food. We want to eat food that lasts — the same way people complain about the sermon with the aching words. "I wanted something to take home with me." People know that suffering is part of life. What we want from our cups is what Jesus drank: the full cup, the one that contains both sorrow and joy.

Many have found life long comfort from the memorization of the Heidelberg catechism... "What is your only comfort in life and death?" "That I belong — body and soul, in life and in death — not to myself but to my faithful savior Jesus Christ." We are fed more by knowing to Whom we belong than by anything else we put in our mouth. The bread and wine of the Holy Table represent this knowledge. It tells us that we belong, body and soul, life and death, to Jesus Christ.

Our contemporary experience is *hunger.* We live in what some people call a time famine (Jerome Segal in *Tikkun,* Winter, 1996). We are spiritually homeless people; we are spiritually hungry people, without even a soup kitchen. These are our faults in the richest country in the world.

Eucharist means fullness of soul and fullness of belonging. Eucharist is the best diet in the world. It both feeds and slims us — in the sense that it right sizes us. Eucharist puts us at table with God and with each other, and there in the slimmest wafer and smallest cup, we find abundant accompaniment. The little is plenty. We mature at the table where food is understood in its depth, as opposed to its speed. When food is understood as a gift to which the only reply is deep thanksgiving, rather than a get which we buy at counters where we hope the help is speedy, Eucharist marks our days. We grow up to the height and depth of the rituals all around us. We feast. We become full instead of "eucharistically starving," as Rosemary Radford Reuther puts it.

Aldous Huxley tells us there are "non-verbal humanities." Once a clown led a group of us unofficially to commune together. She held the bread first as though it were a baby, the baby Jesus. The baby grew and became a cross in her mime. Then the cross poured

48

the blood into the cup. She passed the cup around. This same clown asked us one Christmas to hold a piece of purple cloth and to "make believe" it was the baby Jesus. We could do anything we wanted with it. I held it close to my heart. She wiped the tears of her eyes with it. No one ate it. But they could have.

In a world where it is easy to meet a Zen Christian or a Buddhist-leaning Jew, it is incredible that we still reach for proper ways to have communion. Again, we insult the very people who understand the mystery of table feast and accommodate those who think "Real Presence" is a theological controversy. That Protestants and Catholics don't sit with each other at table shows that the theologians have won the battle of the feast and that they bear major responsibility for how hungry we are.

I think of Nhut's Cafe in Faison, North Carolina. Nhut runs a Vietnamese, Southern-style eatery on the main street of town. Out front are parked dozens of pick-ups every noon. Nhut married a local man when he was a soldier in Vietnam. She has been there for twenty years. Because most of the people are Mexican migrant workers in the fields today, there is salsa on the table, collard greens and egg rolls on the menu. The Real Presence shows up some days and orders the special.

Denise Levertov, the poet, wants to know why we live so hungry in the orchard. What happened to American culture that we could be so hungry in the richest country in the world? Where are our linen tablecloths?

The reason is forgetting to Whom we belong. It has to do with forgetting that real blood was shed at the table where we hold the memorial feast. Good Friday is about real blood, not phony blood. Good Friday is not a spectacle.

Not just the blood of Jesus but the blood of Vietnam Vets and Vietnamese children (just to mention a few of the victims of our amnesia). We live and eat as though the bomb had never fallen, the Jews of Europe had not died, as if Rodney King had not been beaten. We fritter away mystery and awe in paper bags of packaged food.

Let's eat and let us suffer. Let us drink the cup we have been offered.

49

Easter Day

Calmly Plotting
The Resurrection

John 20:1-18

We have come to the end of a spiritual journey, one which we were faithful enough to take. By going all the way through Lent, we come to a new picture for our lives, one that shows how near God is all the time, in every way. We are no longer the center of our life's picture: God is. The stone of us has been rolled away for us.

Stone rollers are in good company. Rock gardeners have the same bargain with eternity: we participate in it. We make changes, ironically, all the time by putting in big sturdy unchanging things. Then we move them or watch their colors change in the rain or their shapes emerge in the snow. Someone said about their own church: "Our continuity here is that we keep changing." Continuity for Christians is the same: the stones keep rolling away from our big and little graves. We enjoy new life every spring in the same way that a gardener enjoys new life. First, things die. Then they live again.

Gardeners participate in a certain seasonal renewal. They count on change, eternally and rigorously. Rock gardeners are not capital R resurrectionists — but they do know a little about the little R. They participate in simple ways in miracles. They watch stones roll away all the time.

Gardeners have enough hope in the future to garden. Christians have enough faith in life after death that we are willing to die. We know that giving up and relinquishing may be a way to receive and grow.

51

One of the most stunning rock sculptures in the nation is at the Jewish Theological Seminary in New York City. Based on the passage from Exodus 16:6 — "Behold, I will stand with you at the rock at Horeb, and you shall strike the rock, and water shall come out of it, that the people may drink" — these sculptures tell the story of the thirst and satisfaction of that verse. Stones roll; water emerges from rock. The Bible is full of "unnatural" things that are really quite natural to God.

Rock and stone are used everywhere in the Bible. Consider Isaiah 26:4: "Trust in the Lord forever, for in the Lord God, you have an everlasting rock." The theme of the rock garden is trust.

If you can't travel to a great rock sculpture, or choose not to, and if you can't make a rock garden or any kind of garden, singing an old hymn can accomplish a simple connection to eternity. You can book a room in eternity for the afternoon. I recommend "Rock Of Ages, Cleft For Me." The interesting part of this hymn is the word "cleft," wherein a little room for you or me is made in eternity.

Everywhere we go, whether to the Great Wall of China; the great castles of Europe; the pyramids of Egypt; the stones of Ireland, Scotland, Wales; the retreat center at Iona; or the biblical literature itself, which put Ten Commandments, supposedly, on real stone, eternity is marked as the rock. Rock is the best metaphor we have of everlastingness, and modern people, in particular, need to place rock around them. We need reminders of how long we, and our children, will last.

As John Vivian puts it so well in his introduction to *Building Stone Walls* (Garden Way Publishing, 1976), "... rock is as near a definition to forever as exists." He credits gravity with keeping rock sitting on top of itself; I credit larger spirits, the spirits within the stones that we use to speak of the permanent, of the way new life always emerges from old. Foundations may be slipping but the rocks are still there, almost begging for the reconnecting spirit of the resurrected householder.

It is no accident that we buy a stone for a loved one who has died and plant small flowers next to it. We don't need to "romance" the stone to know why stone comforts: it stands and it withstands.

It stands and withstands change. It rocks and rolls with us, not against us. That's why.

There is a tremendous shortage of gravemarkers in New England. My own father's stone went on a waiting list for over six months until someone who knew how to carve particularity into eternity could be found. My grandmother's stone wasn't marked 1983, the year of her death, until 1996. That may have been sheer orneriness and inefficiency on the part of the monument company. Then again, a deeper conspiracy may be afoot. Maybe gravemakers are no longer needed. Maybe we don't need to mark graves. Or at least other people's graves. I, for one, want my little bit of eternity marked. By stone. And well-gardened stone. I want someone to remember with me that my death will be followed by new life.

New life is very real to those who know the cancellation of debt. Visit an AA meeting any night of the week, in any community in America. You will hear the stories of canceled debts. These debts are not imagined; they are real. So is the resurrection.

I think of the way E. B. White described his beloved Katherine as she aged but still knelt to plant bulbs in the November wind.

> *As the years went by and age overtook her, there was something comical in her bedraggled appearance — the small hunched-over figure, her studied absorption in the implausible notion that there would be yet another spring, oblivious to the ending of her own days, which she knew perfectly well was near at hand, sitting there with her detailed chart under those dark skies in the dying October, calmly plotting the resurrection.*

In our new picture of a new life, may we be sure that we include a new picture of a new world as well. Now that we have created a new heart within us, let the joy of salvation be restored, everywhere, for everyone.

When we sing the words that beg God to create in us a clean heart, we follow with "restore unto us the joys of thy salvation." How do we know if our sins are forgiven? We know when we enjoy the joys of God's salvation. We know by the lift in our walk.

53

The energy in our vision. The expansion of our sphere of influence. The feeling of being capable of making peace and justice. The hunger for ways to be useful. The grace in our eyes. Our willingness to refrain from whining or accusing or tallying. We are restored to the way God wanted us to be in the first place.

One of the loveliest old prayers, author unknown, called in my life a Pilgrim Prayer, concludes a day with these words:

> *Save me, I pray, for I am still afraid. When I am afraid, I will trust in you. In God whose word I praise, in God I trust; I will not be afraid. You are my hiding place. You will protect me from trouble. You will surround me with songs of deliverance.*

The most difficult thing about repentance is knowing that we may sin again. We may get right back in our own rut again. We may learn of obedience through suffering, the same way Jesus learned it.

I drove to one of our churches with an old friend. We came to a dirt road that was full of spring mud and ruts. A farmer came out of his house and said, "Do you really want to go down that road?" We said, "Yes, it's our favorite back way to the church in Chester. Carol Ann has a little cottage deep in these woods; we're on our way by it up to Chester."

We proceeded down the rutted road as far as we could go — and we had to turn back! We had to back out the whole way, missing the ruts we had already missed. There was no way we were going to make it through.

We both had quite a laugh. We realized we had never turned back at a dangerous road before. We had taken way too many foolhardy risks together. We had a new experience on the way to Chester, one that we will both have to ponder for a long time.

We seemed to like ruts. We seemed to want to be the same over and over again. We seemed to have yet more obedience to learn. And yet more suffering. As we celebrate the resurrection, we may thank God for saving us and reframing us — and we may be sober about our prospects for the future.

Save us, O God, again and again.
Raise us, O God, again and again.
Roll every stone away from every grave we make.

Let us laugh so much, O God, that we become laughter,
Let us sing so much that we become song.
Let us give so much that we become gift.

Through Many Doors, He Comes

John 20:19-31

Jesus came to earth. Jesus left earth. Jesus stays on earth by the power of the Holy Spirit and his disciples.

We know our Savior as a man who went through many incarnations, as a man who walked through many doors. We still know him that way — as someone who comes in and out of our lives.

In *The Man Who Created Narnia: The Story Of C. S. Lewis* by Michael Coran, we see that the popular Christian writer understands his Jesus as a man of many doors. Jesus, according to Lewis, took the ordinary lives of Christians and made them extraordinary, almost mystical. We walk in and out of Jesus' time and space the way Jesus walked in and out of ours.

According to Coran:

> *Plain Jack Lewis lived an ordinary life. His genius emerged early accompanied by the death of his mother when he was a child. He and his brother Warnie made a family into which "Joy," Lewis' only wife, came only briefly towards the end. The humanizing aspects of his life included his pipe and his garden and genuine affection for those who worked for him. Oxford and Cambridge always wondered why he didn't make "more" of himself. The reader will be astonished to see the negative reviews of intellectuals about the Narnia series. Of Lewis' nearly thirty books, at least half were academic and distinguished; the other half have been the lasting gift to humanity. They spoke in plain language about Christianity...."*[1]

Plain language about a transfiguring Christ? Yes. What else could possibly work! Lewis believed in heaven the way he believed in breakfast. To him it was ordinary, "just through that door." "God doesn't want to shut that door; only you can do that."

The now-famous wardrobe through which Edmund, Peter, and Lucy escape to Narnia (and return home safely) came to Lewis through the gift of a child. He was harboring children from London during the war. One of the boys asked what would happen if one went in the wardrobe and tried to come out the other side. Lewis saved that image till mid-life — and put the great Christ Lion, "Aslan on the Move," on the other side.

In his letters, Lewis said, "It is quite useless knocking on the door of heaven for earthly comfort; it's not the sort of comfort they supply there."[2]

Lewis ends his story about Narnia with the children asking, "Dare we? Can it be meant for us? But while they were standing thus a great horn, wonderfully loud and sweet, blew from somewhere inside that walled garden and the gates swung open." Lewis opened many doors for people. He believed in miracles, like they were trains. "Unless you live near a railway, you will not see trains go past your windows." He urged people to let themselves get near wonder and fantasy. He saw the "deeper magic."

Doors go with the resurrection like peanut butter goes with jelly. Painters love to paint doors and windows. They like to make openings in reality, the way Bill Gates couldn't help himself in developing WINDOWS 95, so soon outdated and so soon to be replaced with more windows upon windows upon windows. Everybody loves a door, an opening to new life!

The Hebrew people also worked assiduously on the doors and gates of the Tabernacle. They built beautiful screens, entrances within entrances within entrances. They knew the importance of what was both within and what was beyond.

When we look at the next century, we are standing at the gate. We have many screens to get through. Many apertures. Many openings that don't quite take us where we need to get. We will think we have arrived at the threshold of the new and the renewed, only to find that we have further to go.

Scientists and artists love windows and so do regular people. Whenever I go into someone's house, I go to their windows. I like to look out and see what they can see. My city friends can't see much farther than their neighbor's windows. But they can look out: they can assume the posture of the spiritual adventurer, one who is looking over the horizon, looking to see what God has in mind next.

Georgia O'Keefe in one of her paintings, *Bell, Cross, Ranchos Church, New Mexico*, 1930, put the window and door right smack in the middle of the painting. We have to look *at*, not through them, when we look at this painting. She is trying to say that these openings, these screens, these windows are essential, and not just a small part of reality. According to Barbara Rose, art historian and critic, O'Keefe in this painting tried to change the way we see.

What dare we hope for as the century turns? We may dare to hope to see the way God sees. To see the world as God sees it and not as we do. To see how much God has planned for us. How much God hopes for. How deeply committed God is to getting us to "the other side," the resurrected place.

We may thus dare to be spiritual adventurers who stand tip-toed at the window, looking, watching, waiting, and hoping. There we join the artists and the scientists and the regular people of the world: there we try to see as far and as deeply as we can. We try to change the way we see.

Doors are barriers between inside and outside, danger and safety. Many of us love to cozy up right where we are and shut the doors. We like our safety. But often there is more danger in not opening a door than there is in opening one. Coziness is wonderful, but God also promises movement to us. With God we get safety and adventure, not either but both. God promises an open door: it cannot be shut.

Many of us live so deep in fear that we refuse to leave cramped places. We have a tendency to turn cozy into cramped. We prefer the trouble we know to the trouble we don't know. The adventure in opening doors is a matter of trust: what is on "the other side" is at least as good and comforting as what is here. There may be danger on the other side also; trust lets us take the risk of there being more good and less bad when we open a door. We trust in God's open door. We accept the invitation to adventure.

With Jean Luc Picard in *Star Trek*, we go to places no one has ever been before, like the twenty-first century. With Captain Janeway, also of *Star Trek*, we do all we can to get home. By God's open door policy, we are promised a home in adventure and a home in the future as well as in the past.

The sign language for death is an opening and closing of doors with hands up and down, alternatively, as the image. What is happening as the century turns is that something is both opening and closing. We are saying hello and good-bye. A beginning is an ending.

We hear these sorts of things all the time, especially when others are either trying to console or encourage us. "When one door closes, another opens." The deaf know this fact linguistically. We know it experientially.

Death yields life: when one door closes, another one opens. Ask the people who stood at the sepulchre. The door opened: death became life. Jesus walked into their room.

---

1. *The Man Who Created Narnia: The Story Of C. S. Lewis* by Michael Coran (Eerdmans, 1996), p. 53

2. *Ibid.*, p. 65.

What's For Breakfast?

Luke 24:36b-48

The testimony of Easter is that Jesus joins us again, on earth, after his resurrection from the dead. The disciples make this testimony in at least three ways: on the road to Emmaus, to Mary in the garden, and in our text today, in a request for something to eat for breakfast.

Many people have wished for something larger and more dramatic, only to be given these simple appearances. Many of us also want to be touched by God in our regular life. We await the thunderbolt experience, only to receive the still, small whisper.

A friend tells of a day when she was more than a little beside herself. Life seemed more difficult than she could manage. Even emptying the dishwasher seemed an enormous task. She is not the only one who has ever felt overwhelmed by the details of daily life!

She decided to have a little fun. She took the back road to work, one never taken before, just to give herself a change of pace and look. The road proved circuitous, mountainous, and small! She kept thinking she should turn around, discipline herself to a regular path — and stop being so upset about the dishwasher detail that was frightening her so.

As she turned the final corner to reconnect to the main road, a peacock appeared on the road. The tail feathers were fully displayed. She got the point: Seek and ye shall find; knock and the door shall be open to you. She was able to go to work with a different point of view. The very things that had seemed so large before seemed manageable now. The peacock feathers had put them in

61

their proper size and context, one that included God's magnificent creation — which includes peacocks.

On the way back from France one year, I had a similar experience. We were being served the fancy French lunch that French airlines provide. I looked up to see that the server offering me bread was the pilot. There were his wings, there was his tag, there was his uniform. I panicked a little. "Why aren't you flying the plane?" "Oh," said he, "I needed a change of pace."

When Jesus came to the disciples on the road to Emmaus, he could have said something profound or mysterious. He could have continued as their wisdom figure and once again startled them with his wisdom. Instead, he offered them peace. "Peace be with you." He then asked them what was for breakfast. He made the extraordinary, ordinary.

A little religion goes a long way. I think of cults and the way they magnify the wisdom and peace of Jesus beyond all proportion. Heaven's Gate, for example, took everything that major religions say about life and overdid it. New Age and up-to-the-technological minute, they still got trapped by the oldest sin of all: pride. Like true believers everywhere, Heaven's Gate flew too close to the sun of their own certainty.

Religions of all types see eternity as a continuation of the present moment. They make the ordinary, extraordinary, and vice versa. They take breakfast dishes and place them in the proper context. I think of the Celtic sense of thin or transparent moments, when heaven and earth blend a bit, in an ecstatic experience. In C. S. Lewis' *The Lion, The Witch, And The Wardrobe*, the children go through a simple door, and there is as an opening to a simultaneous world. Lewis swore that death was just "opening a door." Many of us believe he was right. We don't need to kill ourselves to be picked up by a spaceship.

Where cults go wrong is in their idolatrous appropriation of religious metaphors: they think they know more than God about when heaven and earth intersect. They get too smart. In genuine religious experiences, people become more humble and open. The captain serves bread. But the phony close time: they think they know what God is doing and give themselves the lead in God's script.

Religions of all types do advocate that we write ourselves into the divine script. "I am the Way, the Truth, and the Life," said Jesus. "Follow me." Remembering that we are not God is the trick that lets people be actors in God's holy play. When we confuse ourselves with God and decide that our chariot is coming on a certain day, at a certain time, we move ourselves to a place that looks a lot like heaven but is actually hell. We get like our friend was before she saw the peacock: we occupy too much of the space in our life and forget that the world is larger than our preoccupations.

The hell is aggravated self-control. Genuine religion keeps God in charge of the important stuff, like life and death and appointments with chariots. Genuine religion is, as those now dead believed too hard and too well, a kind of surrender. The devil is tricky: the devil can twist even the good of surrender into the evil of controlling appointments with God.

As established religions become more boring, and more status quo oriented, cults thrive. They thrive by the simple act of coloring a grey world. Established religions, both Jewish and Christian, are more and more obsessed with our own institutional survival. We spend too much of our time being anxious about "why people don't come to church or synagogue any more," thereby creating exactly the scene we are trying to avoid. Pride and self-absorption twist good into evil.

The Divine is divine because it cannot be manipulated either by anxious establishments or by appointments made on-line for end time. When Jesus chooses to join us on our ride, or on our airplane, Jesus will. He will come as bread or breakfast. He will come simply, as he has done before.

When we try to control God with our grandiose fantasies of what God ought to be, we miss the God of the garden, or the God of breakfast, or the God of bread and wine. We miss the God made known to us in the breaking of the bread.

There is a little bit of the cultic and the desire for the dramatic in each of us. We want God to be the star of stage and screen — but God chose to come as a humble man, a carpenter's son, one identified fully with the little people. God made a grand world of peacocks and comets and airlines — but chose for best embodiment, a child, a man, a simple one at that.

Little people know that the grace of God is at the core of the universe. We open doors but don't close them on God. We remember how long a way a little goes. We enjoy comets. We don't ride them. We worship a God who comes for breakfast, who doesn't need a three-star restaurant but actually prefers walking with us at the beach.

During this Easter season we need more to right-size our expectations of God — not downsize them but right-size them. When we are ready to let the ordinary be extraordinary, we will probably receive a visit, just like the disciples did. Thus will the scriptures be opened to us.

The Culture
Of Disbelief

John 10:11-18

What does this shepherd possibly mean? He says he has the power to put his life down and to pick it up again! It is almost like he is saying we can stop breathing whenever we want — and then begin breathing again. How dare we believe this promise?

Especially how dare we believe this promise in a world which has made a culture out of disbelief or suspicion? Just think of yourself in front of the television. Thin thighs in thirty days. Ha! Beautiful chicken in ten minutes. Ha, ha! Most beautiful music in the world. Only $10.99 per month. We have been tutored to disbelief, especially in grand promises. Especially when a shepherd comes along and says death can go to life and back to death and then back to life!

The shepherd of the everlasting life promise (or advertisement) says he has the *power*. The power to do what he says he can do. The chicken/thigh/music people don't have the power. They just say that they do. Jesus says he has the power.

In the widely read book *The Culture Of Disbelief,* Stephen Carter says:

> *Religions ... (as aliens) are not simply a means of understanding one's self, or even of contemplating the nature of the universe, or existence, or of anything else. A religion is, at its heart, a way of denying the authority of the rest of the world. Religions are exercises in resistance ... religions reveal various possibilities for*

human freedom. It is really an alien way of knowing the world.

Similarly, Noam Chomsky, writing in the *Nation* magazine, speaks of the way multinational corporations encourage cynicism about government. That cynicism releases them from pressure and observation. It keeps countervailing force from amassing.

The similarity is in the way government turns on religion: government understands that religion is a test of its ultimate authority. It tests governmental authority "epistemologically." Religion says government does have authority but not idolatrous or ultimate authority.

False power or aggrandized power works falsely. We need to understand how the assumptions of false power work. They work to hurt us, the same way wasting our money on quick chicken recipes that don't taste good hurts us. They hurt our capacity for trust. When the truly good Shepherd does come along, we have forgotten how to believe. We are too hurt in our centers of trust to believe.

When we undermine trust in things, we attack them at their centers. The center of institutions is their ability to maintain trust. The center of parenting is its ability to maintain trust. The center of a marriage is the same. When we undermine trust in things, we find the stuffing gone from us. We are limp. We are weak. We can't find our way forward.

What has happened to the churches of America? We have not been able to maintain trust. Our people think we do things that they don't want or that represent their faith falsely. Indeed "large" or "wide" structures have not been trustworthy; they have moved outside the circle of influence and trust of their members. Study after study shows that denominational leaders follow a different gospel than people in the pews. It has also been in the interest of governmental and economic structures to undermine the capacity of religion to challenge their authorities publicly.

The devil is not foolish. The devil is smart. The devil is a wolf that steals and devours the sheep. The devil doesn't need big

66

weapons when small disappointments will do to undermine larger capacities for trust.

How could we restore trust to a church system, or to religion, or to government, marriage or family? We restore faith by behaving in a trustworthy way. How do religious institutions behave in trustworthy ways? Religious institutions are trustworthy by making sure their own power is subservient to their primary interest, which is their mission, and by making sure we love our children more than we love our so-called responsibility or authority over them.

Jesus loved the sheep. That was his power. He genuinely loved the sheep, so much so that he was willing and able to do whatever was needed to protect them — even to die in the process. The way he came second to the sheep was his power and his authority.

For example, if the conference for which I work tries to maintain itself institutionally (a normal enough institutional tendency) more than it tries to strengthen its member parishes, it loses trust. The opposite is also true. If member parishes don't try to strengthen their membership one with another, they sacrifice the strength of the wider system, which is their power to keep God in centrality and large human systems out of oppressive, idolatrous powers.

Kenotic, or self-emptying, power is the trick. We might even call it the Palm Sunday trick, or the Easter trick. Losing power is the way we gain trust. Trust is more important than power. Losing ourselves is the way we gain ourselves.

I heard a story about a grandmother who danced with her grandson at a wedding. The grandson didn't know how to dance. The grandmother did. Sounds like a familiar generational pattern, doesn't it? The boy had heard somewhere that if you just "cinch 'em up tight" they enjoyed the dance, even if you were faking half the steps. The grandmother knew exactly what was going on as she glided across the floor, breathing more and more from the upper diaphragm. At first, she thought about improving the boy's steps. But out of love for him, and respect for his clumsy love for her, she just closed her eyes. "I dreamed," she said, "that he was a great dancer ... and I knew he wasn't dancing with me." And, of course, he was. Love carries the day that skill can't. Trust carries us when some facts fail.

We sometimes have to dance even when disappointed at the skill of our partner. We have to trust our way beyond disappointments in trust. So many of the attempts we make at loving each other are like a kite that gets caught in a telephone pole. We miss our flight. We get stuck. We can't get unstuck. Those who have been hurt have a hard time trusting — but we can limp along or dance as well as we can without good breathing!

How do we learn to pick up our life after it has been stuck somewhere? We must only love, only let go, only die a little, let the death be. It is not the important thing. What is important is getting unstuck to love again. What is important is being able to dance, anyway.

A little boy was outside his seaside parish in England, making a sand castle at the gate of the church. The Bishop came for a visit. Thinking he could quickly charm the child and all who were watching him charm the child, thinking he could make a big hit in a small place, he asked the child what he was making. The boy said, "A cathedral."

"Oh," said the Bishop, "where is the bishop for your cathedral?" "I don't have enough dirt for a bishop, Sir."

Perhaps we can leave Jesus' promise right there. When we leave ourselves out of it, we are more able to put ourselves in to it. When we put ourselves into it, we find that we are put out. The good shepherd knows his sheep. The good shepherd uses his power to know his sheep. In this way, love is all the power we need. It is our cathedral, our dance, our glide, our kite, our guide. What we give up, we may have. What we fail to give up, we lose.

Vining And Branching

John 15:1-8

Parents know exactly what Jesus means about vining and branching. We know the connection of fruiting to pruning, the connection of fruiting to watering, the deep relationship we have with our children. There are consequences to our abilities to love them. If we can love them, they can mature and bear fruit. If we cannot love them, they cannot mature and bear fruit.

Jesus speaks of God as his Father, the vinegrower. He attributes his ability to fruit to his parent. How does he fruit? He abides in God. We have the same choice, the same good news, the same capacity for maturity and fruiting.

I am always amazed by the myth of individualism! We really do imagine that we make ourselves when in fact we make each other. Our parents make us and then we make our children. God made Jesus who makes, and remakes, us. We have tremendous personal, if not individual, responsibility for ourselves: we make choices about which environment we choose to form us. Even if there is failure in pruning and watering and caring, God can enter our lives. God can relove us. God can relove our children. One of the meanings of the resurrection is right here: we are given another chance to love each another. We may rechoose the spiritual environment in which we grow.

Dominick Crossan, the New Testament scholar, says that Christians often mistake sin and salvation as matters of individual choice. They are not. They are matters of social or group choice. Both sin and salvation are systemic; they are system-wide. They are like the vine and the branches: things connect in our world. In relationships and connections, things are what they are.

Individual choice matters so much precisely because it is part of the vining and branching. When we choose to disconnect from God, the vinegrower, and begin to act as though we can manage ourselves, we die.

Salvation begins with God's choice to save the world through Jesus, and ends with our personal and communal choices to say yes to that choice, to allow ourselves to be reloved and remade and reborn, over and over again.

Specific moral choices will show what I mean. I think of "Sunday Morning Soccer" and what pastors and churches and parents can do both to open and to protect our "slot." I think of the battle we have about whether it takes a "village" or a family to raise a child, when obviously it takes both. What matters is how we create environments that branch salvation to our children.

On the one hand, churches must defend our Sabbath time. On the other, we must find ways to include youth in worship times that are more friendly to their actual life and commitments.

Sports are not so much a leisure activity as a sacred activity. It is not accidental that they occupy "prime time." What churches must face in the competition for our once sacred slot is that we aren't speaking the holy in a language people can understand.

Our loss of cultural dominance is nowhere so visibly seen as in the competition over Sunday mornings. This lost imperialism is both a positive and a negative. For too long that imperialism worked as a kind of tenure: we thought we had it made and therefore didn't "work" very hard to make sense of our message. We became civil servant employees of the gospel. (No, not all tenured faculty slack off once secure, nor do all civil servants abuse their security. But the churches did.) Now that we have to make plain our vision we are better off. It was harmful to the gospel itself to have it so firmly supported by culture.

Religion is not individual choice. And I *do* say that as a parent raising children in two magnificent faith traditions. We are not setting our children up for choice so much as immersing them. We are stewing them! We are depending on the village and the parish and the synagogue to help us raise the children. We want them to be deep enough inside religious tradition that they can see the magnificent vining and branching that is going on, by the action of God in history.

Jews assumed they would be sidelined by culture. They assume lots of activities on Saturdays. Their religion had none of the chutzpah of Christianity. Christianity is fast on its way to becoming more "Jewish." We too have to make our case to the world. We too are a genuine alternative to culture's sense of religion, including most basicly American culture's myth of individualism.

There is great advantage in having to make our vine visibly fruit in front of our children. We have to make our argument over and over and to make it well. Why *do* we love Jesus?

The negative side of these advantages lies in the simple surplus of choices that the modern family faces. A pastor in a small hill town north of here said, "I don't think I could face the daily stress my fifteen-year-old faces." What stress is there in Shelburne Falls, we might ask? The same stress that is in the big cities: the stress is the surplus of stimulation.

People argue that the average person today negotiates fifteen times as much stimulation as people in a previous era. Children multiply that stimulation by the kinds of games and television they watch. Getting them to choose between a patterned, Sabbathed life and a jumpy chaotic menu is stressful. Ask the soccer moms. Consider the difference between a rooted vine twisted around an old arbor — place that image in your mind as an image of the kind of salvation Jesus promised. Then replace that image with energy on a screen. You will begin to see two versions of systems. You will begin to see the world our children see. They see *both* the old images and the new images. Their world of images is at least doubled!

Another loss, beyond the management of surplus choices, is the loss of sacred or "enchanted" time. Time becomes all the same when a culture refuses to enjoy a Sabbath, whether Saturday or Sunday.

The church has a stake in sacred time — even more a stake than it has in its time slot. We have a stake in getting our message

71

to our children: that time is sacred, that God is real and involved in our history, that Jesus Christ has saved us, and that "it's not all up to us."

When we remember the message of Jesus about the vines and the branches, we are really only hearing common sense, religiously spoken. One parent all by himself or herself cannot change the environment our children live in. If parents really want to do something about Sunday mornings and about a more patterned and less stressful time, the solution is fairly simple. It is a secular solution. We have to organize the soccer moms and players in our group. If one speaks, nothing will happen. In my experience, if several speak, children not showing up for Sunday practices will not result in sports penalties and not being able to play. There is also an important community conversation that happens when "time" becomes a subject. The church acts for God, and God's sacralizing message, instead of on behalf of its "slot."

"Abide in me as I abide in you," said Jesus. "Apart from me you can do nothing." But with him, and with each other, we can do everything. We can grow to our full maturity in Christ, as can our children.

On The Matter Of Love

John 15:9-17

The presence of God is the difference between joy and happiness. We can be happy without God but we may not be joyful without God.

Jesus promised joy when he said, "I have come that your joy might be increased ..." (John 15:11 and 10:10). He came by way of the cross which leads to joy and not just happiness.

Happiness is a checkbook that has money, a car that works, a good date for Saturday night. Happiness is the absence of major hassles or terrorism or crime; happiness is children getting good report cards and one's spouse getting a raise. Happiness is something we know as enhancement or protection of our own lives.

Joy comes in the connection with an other or with Jesus. Joy comes as presence with God or as simply the presence of God. Joy can happen without money or a working car. Joy happens when we get to the core of life and realize that love is at the core. Joy befriends us; love accompanies us.

I know a woman who has four children. Three have AIDS. She does too. Her only hope is to outlive her three dying children so that she can comfort them as they leave this earth. She calls these dying children "morning glories." The name seems to be catching on for children who have AIDS. Their life is brief but beautiful. This woman knows almost no happiness, but God is never far away from her. She knows the joy of the presence of God. Her fourth son, she says, will have to be taken care of by the future. I asked her where she got her faith, and she said that she had no idea but that without it she'd already be dead. With it, at least she can enjoy what she calls the morning's glory.

She loves these children — for whatever moment they have. Jesus loves us that way: joyously, for now, fully in the present. Love can be there even if a future or a good report card is not. Joy can be there in spite of terrible grief or loss or hassles. Neither love nor Jesus is destroyed in terrorism. Ask the people of Oklahoma City or any of the parents who lost a child: they know that weeping endures for the night but joy comes in the morning.

A completed joy comes in spite of the terrible losses. An old woman once confessed to me that she worried about people who had never suffered until late in life: "They don't know about tomorrow and how we get over things." Joy comes when we are healed by the power and presence of God which is even more present in acute suffering. The score is always God 10-Suffering 9 or God 11-Suffering 10. Suffering can be horrible, but God is always more powerful than any suffering.

Jesus did not live and die to make us happy so much as to yield us joy. Joy is inclusive; happiness is often exclusive. Joy comes to people who lose legs or children or jobs. Happiness comes to the competent and the fortunate: joy has its arms around everybody.

Consider this parable about poor people. It could also be titled "The Strange Way the Cookie Crumbles." A rich woman found herself with some time to spare at London's Heathrow Airport. She bought a cup of coffee and a small bag of cookies. She staggered, laden with luggage, to an unoccupied table. She was reading the morning paper when she became aware that a very shabbily dressed man was seated at her table, eating a cookie. She did not want to make a scene so she leaned across and took a cookie herself. A minute or so passed. More rustling. He was helping himself to another cookie! The back and forth continued until they were down to the last cookie in the package. She was very angry but still could not bring herself to say anything. Then the young man broke the remaining cookie in two, pushed half across to her, ate the other half and left.

Some time later, when the public address system called for her to present her ticket, she was still fuming. Imagine her embarrassment when she opened her handbag and was confronted by her package of cookies! She had been eating his.

He was rich enough to share. She was not. He knew about joy. She only knew about cookies.

If joy is not something you know intimately, perhaps God will send you some suffering or some poverty. Even better — because who could wish for suffering for anyone — you might consider behaving as a wave of joy. You might spread the joy you do know. Joy *does not* only come to those who suffer; it also comes to those who get acquainted with who God really is.

Consider *the wave*. Not an Atlantic Ocean wave but the sporting event wave. Who starts it? How do 14,000 people get going all together in something like a rhythm? Somebody must start it. So why not you or me? The person who starts it is who starts it. When it starts, people get receptive to taking instruction. People cooperate. We experience what the computer types call a positive feedback loop. Everything is amplified. We don't have any special power but we experience joy anyway. Waves really show you the difference between power and effect. In lots of situations, we don't really have any power. But we can have a big effect if the situation is set up right.

A small amount of power can have a large effect Somebody starts every wave. Every joy and every love starts somewhere. It doesn't just happen. Somebody starts every wave.

Next time you are at a dinner party and everyone starts making themselves feel good by putting down the people who aren't there, watch what happens if you stop that wave and offer a replacement. Or watch the next fight you have with your spouse or children or neighbor. The same principle applies. Harness the positive power in the situation and you may diffuse the negative. You might even have a big effect. You might even find the effect of your action magnified. You might even start to have a good time!

You probably don't think you have what it takes to start waves of joy. But you do. Rabbits prove it.

We found the rabbits on a street in Vermont. The sign said, "Freeeee bunies." My children were young and went into an immediate sit-down strike in front of the "freeeee bunies." I argued that they would never survive the winter. My argument fell on deaf ears. Guess what? They did survive the winter. How? By growing fur as they needed it.

Our capacity for joy is the same. We grow the fur as we need it, depending on how cold it actually gets. Christ stays close to suffering. There is no growth or blockage, blood or gore, that Christ cannot penetrate and use for strength within us. Nothing can separate us from the Love of God. Even more powerfully true is this fact: God gives us what we need as we need it. God does not need to use suffering to show us joy, but God can. God 12- Suffering 11 is the end score of every important life game. But why wait for suffering when we can wave with joy right now? God's presence gives us what we need when we need it.

What do we need? Just joy. Just love. That's all. That's all.

Stay In
The City

Luke 24:44-53

When Jesus leaves earth, in the Ascension, he advises that we stay in the city. We don't know everything we are going to know yet. We are not yet clothed with "power from on high." We will be. But we're not there yet. Jesus' advice in the meantime, or mid-time, between his leaving and his return, is that we stay where we are.

He is talking out of a rich sense of time. It is not the kind of advancing, clock-type time in which you and I live. He is talking about eternity and the way his incarnation in time has happened and will happen again.

There may be just a thousand days left in the century, but I doubt that it matters. I will wake up the first day of the new century with unknit yarn, unfolded laundry, unreturned phone calls, the same extra ten pounds of flesh. For me, time is continuous, cyclical, almost folk. For those who tell me about time, it is digital, advancing, and "modern." I save a certain hesitancy. I am suspicious of time that is not waiting for the return of its origin, for "God to come again in glory."

Time doesn't make sense without a beginning and an end. Digital time insults the good time of God which has a beginning and an end which are connected to each other.

I think I am as modern as the next soldier in Progress' conscientiously objecting army. Many of us resemble the Mexican woman who announced, "By day, I am Christian. At night, I dance." With Marcia Clark, by day, we wear our angel pins and on Sundays say our rosaries or sing our sophisticated doxologies. We swear we believe in the Trinity. We also cry in movies. There are those who will say these very mixtures are the post part of our modern culture. I bet my mother was fairly good at blending too. I don't mean that I don't believe in the Trinity: rather I mean that I believe in it and angels too, side by side, in a blend that is the best version of my city that I can come up with. I blend God's kind of time and culture's kind of time, all the time.

We blend city and God's city all the time, in many ways. We may believe in God's sense of continuous time but we also wear a watch. We make appointments and get to them (somewhat) "on time."

When Jesus advises that we stay in the city during this interim period, between his first and second coming, I think he means that we stay in time. That we live in our kind of time, our kind of city.

When we live in time, we live with our unfinishedness. We learn to be in process. We learn what it means to want to become new and not know how. What if you were sick of yourself, your house, your clothes, and your car, but were too old to take off for the West Coast in a jalopy? What if you had heard just one too many stories about the crash of currency in Indonesia and couldn't stand to worry about your own problems any more? But what if you didn't stop worrying about your own problems? What if a new part of you was struggling to be born, to shed an old skin, to find a new way — but you felt wrapped tightly in shrink wrap, like a sandwich that has stayed on the shelf too long, waiting to be chosen, waiting to be used up, waiting to be discovered? Finally, all the customers go home and there you are, still on the shelf, still in a holding pattern. Shrunk. Wrapped.

Or you are an airplane circling over the airport. Air traffic control says wait your turn. You can't go down; you have to stay up. Others got here before you. But you could run out of fuel. You have told air traffic control that if you have to stay in this pattern one more circle, you might crash. They don't respond.

Or you are the pastor of a congregation that patterns itself after yesterday. You preach tomorrow; it lives yesterday. You wonder if what you do matters. You don't see the security of Sunday on Tuesday night in the board meeting. You live but you don't thrive.

You preach or hear a whole sermon on substituting the word "responsibility" for the word "fault" — and then go to the annual meeting of the parish and the first three speakers say something that was not done or poorly done is their "fault."

Many of us are sure that God is a part of this kind of time as well as part of "perfect" or improved time. We see God as at least one step ahead of the devil. We know that even cyberspace has a heaven and a hell. We know the sacred part of present and past.

The Holy Spirit is on the Internet, if in no other place than the ways parents and children talk with each other daily again, after long separations. People are able to be closer to their families because of the Internet. People are able to find out after plane crashes what happened and to do so quickly. People are able to inquire after each other when a flood comes to a village they used to live in. They can get there quickly; they can ask what is happening to those they love. I have an e-mail relationship with a woman in China! Dare I imagine that God is not behind these good things that happen in our city? They seem to me to be part of the coming of God's time and God's commonwealth, what we called God's kingdom when that was the type of city people lived in.

Those of us who know the pattern of the Holy Spirit are not surprised. We know how Spirit breaks through nooks and crannies, webs and nets. We know how Spirit gets where it wants to get, even when "modern" has banned it from using the front door.

The Holy Spirit joins the devil in working pre- and post-modern, pre- and post-millennium. Children learn how to build bombs on the Internet. They also learn to know other cultures. Sometimes the Spirits are good; sometimes they are not. Often we are too naive to know the difference.

Jesus said, "Stay in the city," after he rose from the dead. He doesn't mean that we are alone. The Holy Spirit stays with us.

Sometimes our silence is more powerful than our speech. We may need to comment less on the seeming all powerful nature of the modernity blanket. We may need to let it make its own case.

Virginia Owens puts my strategy well. It is the quiet, sure hope in a miracle to topple modernity's conceit. She says:

The sustained existence of the church has always been by miracle ... Augustine died during the siege of Hippo: things could not have looked good. It will be interesting to see how the Almighty pulls this one off.

I'm not talking about trivial or well-promoted quiet, like that small tasteful sign which says that American Express "donated" the plaque at the Hidden Temple in Beijing. I am talking about things we say to each other when we really talk. I mean authentic speech and sharing with our God and with each other.

When we tell each other in truth what is really going on in our real time, we reframe ourselves. A new frame is a new picture. A reorientation of the material. A new frame is a kind of resurrection, or resuscitation. Or renewal. It is as good as a new outfit, as fresh as a haircut that works, as lively as a well-set table awaiting a well-cooked meal.

Writer Tillie Olson spoke of her life needing margin. It had run into the walls of her frame. Artists and photographers insist that the empty space around an object defines it as much as the colored-in part. Our journey through Lent and Easter is the rearrangement of the space in which we live. It is a look at context, at the air, at the nothing that is ours. We have the opportunity to live deeper in our time on behalf of God's time. We stay in the city of time and space waiting for God.

Christ has died, Christ has risen, Christ will come again.

Sanctified In The Truth

John 17:6-19

When Jesus prays for his disciples, he asks that they be sanctified in the truth. Made holy by the truth. Freed by the truth. What he says in a very complex sermon (for Jesus) is that the truth is relationship. We don't belong to the world. Nor does Jesus belong to the world. We belong to God.

The truth is relationship to God. This sanctifying truth is very hard to understand in a world like ours, which sanctifies individualism and isolation and discrete parts. We don't really believe in relationship, theoretically or practically. We believe in breaking things down into their constituent parts. We dissect to know. We imagine that we are on our own in the universe. Jesus connects to know: he knows that we are not alone.

Ask the new welfare policy: it lives by the ethic of personal responsibility, not collective relationship. Or ask the school teacher who discovers children cooperating on their work: grades are still given to individuals, not to groups.

The case of Richard Jewell and the media shows how we see individuals and individualism. Jewell, suspected by the FBI and a media feeding frenzy of the pipe-bombing at the Atlanta Summer Olympics, woke up a private person and went to bed a public person. He was both public and private at dawn and public and private at dusk — but his self-understanding shifted. He had to go to court to complain about just how public his private side became.

His case against his offenders rests not on his claim of libel so much as on whether he will be judged as a public or a private person. Libel laws protect public people even more than they protect private people. Why? Because public people need room in which to maneuver, or so think the writers of the law.

They may be right about the necessity of additional protection for public speech. Legal life has some important differences from real life: in real life, we need to depend on both common sense and justice. Not just one, but both. Common sense tells all Americans that we only look more public and more private at any given moment. We are always both public and private, both individual and grouped, both isolated and connected, all the time. In a world where spiritual wisdom insists on relationship, and actual life teaches individualism, we are always being buffeted by dual longings and dual messages. Richard Jewell is not alone.

Consider just how many issues turn on this point about public and private, isolated or connected. Jewell may choose to behave as if he were "just" a private or public person. But we all know that security guards wake up in the morning to public responsibilities. Their person affects their profession. Their profession surely affects their person, as well. Ask the wife of any policeman how private her husband's life is.

Conservatives image welfare reform as though there was an individual somewhere who by virtue of personal responsibility could find a job that doesn't exist. Liberals counteract from their side of the partiality: their take on welfare is that of the necessity of collective intervention on behalf of victimized individuals. Any fool can see that systemic reform coupled with personal responsibility will yield welfare reform. Not either, but both. Relationship will prevail — especially if Republicans and Democrats figure out how to have one!

The charitable choice provision of the new welfare reform bill — in which religious institutions can get government help to provide for the poor — is a marvelous improvement on the old separation of church and state. If only religious institutions help the poor, however, their help will also fall on the sword of the dangerous public/private dichotomy. Religious institutions will be no more moral when faced with large public grants than others have been. We need not just private institutions or public institutions but both.

82

We need private accountability for public money and public ways to keep individuals accountable.

Think of the Hillary Clinton/Bob Dole flap over village and family. One paraded the more public; the other the more private. Both have to know that you can parent children at your optimum and bad coaches or teachers or Sunday school superintendents can do in years of nurture. It takes both a village and a family to raise children. Not either, but both.

Richard Jewell innocently represents a picture of the dichotomy in our comfortable, if inadequate, self-image. A used-car salesman keeps telling his public that he is a self-made man. People know, however, that he inherited the car dealership from his father. Many position the "private sector" as independent of costly public infrastructure in the same way. Let Microsoft try to make money without publicly-built phone lines or let entrepreneurs make profits without roads for a while just to get the full dimension of the myth of privacy. Consider what the GI bills did to create the suburbs we now resell, property by property, at higher personal profits.

Richard Jewell is "Any Man" — who woke up in the morning and tried to do his job and discovered, if he didn't know already, that he was part of the larger world. His person and his private life are now affected by his being in the wrong place at the wrong time. While we want justice for him as a person, we also want fair self-descriptions of ourselves as a people. We want both. Not either.

Jesus helps us "fix" this awful dichotomy which not only Jewell faces but which we all will face. He says that we belong, both as individuals and as communities, not just to each other but also to God. He actually speaks of getting the right theory of our life correct as "making our joy complete." We find ourselves not alone, and not just in relationship with each other, but each and both contained in a larger, more full relationship with God who made us — and, as the old commentaries insist, "not we see ourselves." When we move beyond the dichotomies of our ways of seeing, we begin to see ourselves as God sees us. God sees us as belonging, as moving toward a completed joy. God sees us as not alone but connected, both to each other and to God.

Books In This Cycle B Series

GOSPEL SET
A God For This World
Sermons for Advent/Christmas/Epiphany
Maurice A. Fetty

The Culture Of Disbelief
Sermons For Lent/Easter
Donna E. Schaper

The Advocate
Sermons For Sundays After Pentecost (First Third)
Ron Lavin

Surviving In A Cordless World
Sermons For Sundays After Pentecost (Middle Third)
Lawrence H. Craig

Against The Grain — Words For A Politically Incorrect Church
Sermons For Sundays After Pentecost (Last Third)
Steven E. Albertin

FIRST LESSON SET
Defining Moments
Sermons For Advent/Christmas/Epiphany
William L. Self

From This Day Forward
Sermons For Lent/Easter
Paul W. Kummer

Out From The Ordinary
Sermons For Sundays After Pentecost (First Third)
Gary L. Carver

Wearing The Wind
Sermons For Sundays After Pentecost (Middle Third)
Stephen M. Crotts

Out Of The Whirlwind
Sermons For Sundays After Pentecost (Last Third)
John A. Stroman

SECOND LESSON SET
Humming Till The Music Returns
Sermons For Advent/Christmas/Epiphany
Wayne Brouwer

Ashes To Ascension
Sermons For Lent/Easter
John A. Stroman